INT

MW00527346

"Christ wishes to enter our lives."

Ever since the Last Supper, the Eucharist has been the church's most beloved treasure—the source and the summit of our life as Catholics. But when we do something Sunday after Sunday, it's easy to let routine take over. It's easy to take the meaning and the power and the promise of Eucharist for granted.

"Eucharist," Pope Francis says, "is essential, because it is Christ's chance to come to us and fill us with grace." The U.S. bishops have made a Eucharistic Revival the center of their strategic plan, "Created Anew by the Body and Blood of Christ, Source of Our Hope," so that all Catholics may regain a sense of the centrality of Eucharist in our lives.

In line with the bishops' call to renew the church, this booklet offers thirty days of reflections on the Eucharist inspired by Pope Francis' words, a journey of discovery to open our eyes and hearts to a new appreciation of what we do when we celebrate this greatest of mysteries.

The quotes from Pope Francis were chosen
by Deborah McCann, who also wrote the reflections
and the "Ponder" and "Pray" pieces.

Cover photo: M.MIGLIORATO/CPP/CIRIC

ISBN 978-1-62785-210-4 ■ Printed in the U.S.A.

1 | MEDICINE, NOT REWARD

*We come to Eucharist not to receive a prize
for being perfect but to receive the medicine
and nourishment we need.*

Pope Francis stunned the world early in his papacy
by identifying himself first and foremost as a sinner
in constant need of God's grace. In the Eucharist, he
says, we have chance after chance to meet God face
to face and to be healed and fed. Eucharist is not a
reward for good deeds done. It is rather the nourishment our sometimes jaded and overwhelmed spirits
need to regain their strength. To be filled with God's
grace is our aim every time we gather. And God is
always ready to meet us, feed us, and hold us close!

PONDER

Do I come to Mass consciously in need of healing?
What nourishment do I need from God today?

PRAY

God of mystery and wonder, help me to approach
your table with awe and humility.

2 | WHAT DO WE GATHER FOR?

Why do we go to Sunday Mass? Are we seeking affirmation, or something more?

Pope Francis seldom speaks of "going to" Mass, but rather of "living" it. He expects us to be active participants in the unfolding liturgical action. We all come to Mass with needs, wants, and hopes—that's a given. But when we gather in community, our own personal intentions give way to something bigger than what's on our minds. We are asking for the grace to move beyond ourselves—grace to live our lives better, to love our families more, to be more honest and more faith-filled than when we entered—so that we may bring Christ to the world. We're not looking for a pat on the back, but for God's strength.

PONDER
Is there someone I can pray for at Mass that I might not have considered before?

PRAY
God of mystery and wonder, help me lay my needs aside, so that I may be open to do your will!

3 | CONSIDERING OTHERS

In the Eucharist, Christ is constantly renewing his gift of self, the gift that he gave on the cross.

Pope Francis reminds us that Jesus loved being with others. He loved his disciples, and he loved the people who gathered around him. No one escaped his attention, and he was always moved and energized by people's hopes and dreams and problems. He learned what stirred people's souls. When we're at Mass, do we really see the people around us? Do we see everyone as equally loved by God? Jesus loved us all so much that he died for us, an action we remember every time we gather. Our first task when we come together is always to consider others. We're all God's children.

PONDER
Is there someone I can get to know at church that I've never talked with before?

PRAY
God of mystery and wonder, remind me always of all the people you hold in your heart!

4 | TO SEE OR BE SEEN

After Mass, how do I live the call to help others?
Do I try to help, or am I somewhat indifferent?
Or do I come ready to find fault and complain?

Pope Francis has a keen eye for the real world that the church is part of. He's completely aware that some people love to gossip or find fault with everything in the church—decorations, music, homilies, the parking lot, and, most of all, other worshipers. And he uses some blunt language: "This should not happen!" Our parishes are made up of people from different economic, social, cultural, and linguistic backgrounds, but all are equally beloved of God. We are fed at Mass in order that we may feed others. How can we improve our response to this call?

PONDER
Do I come to church "armed" or with open arms?

PRAY
God of mystery and wonder, heal me of my impulse to judge and to find fault. Help me to see with eyes of mercy and love.

5 | FORGIVE ME, LORD, FOR I HAVE SINNED

We come to Mass because we are sinners and we want to receive God's pardon, to participate in Jesus' redemption and forgiveness.

One of the first things we do at Mass, Pope Francis reminds us, is ask for forgiveness. And this shouldn't be just words but an actual act of penitence. "We must go to Mass humbly, like sinners, and the Lord forgives us," he says. The blessing that follows is a great act of reconciliation, not just with God, but with one another. What a powerful way to begin! By acknowledging both our sinfulness and God's power to forgive, we are prepared to participate that much more fully, all of us together!

PONDER

How can I more deeply celebrate the reconciliation the Lord offers?

PRAY

God of mystery and wonder, help me to be conscious of all the ways you reach out to me!

6 | AN ACT OF CHRIST

The mission and the very identity of the church flow from the Eucharist.

Pope Francis reminds us that we do not make the Eucharist happen. It is not *our* action, but rather God's action, with Christ himself coming to be with us, to be part of our lives. This is very important, because it is what connects the liturgical action with our daily lives. When we take up the call to act as Christ does in all that we do, we keep enacting this connection every day. As Pope Francis says, our celebrations may be technically and ritually flawless, but if they do not lead us to encounter Jesus Christ, they are "unlikely to bear any kind of nourishment to our heart and our life."

PONDER
How can I be sure to consciously connect liturgy with my life?

PRAY
God of mystery and wonder, increase my awareness of your presence everywhere!

7 | AT THE SERVICE OF LIFE
AND COMMUNION

*When Jesus, through his compassion and love,
giv<us a grace, forgives us our sins, embraces us,
loves us, he does all this completely.*

"All were satisfied." In reflecting on the story of the
loaves and the fish, Pope Francis emphasizes that
it was far more than physical nourishment that the
people received. The people were filled with Christ's
love and compassion, filled with his grace. Even his
disciples were suddenly awakened to what he was
really asking of them. It is this dimension of being
fed that we should ponder every time we receive
communion—am I ready to share this grace and
bounty with others, with everyone?

PONDER
Does receiving communion fill my heart with
God's love and grace?

PRAY
God of mystery and wonder, help me to realize all
the ways you are feeding me each day!

8 | YOU GIVE THEM SOMETHING TO EAT

The Lord meets our needs, but he wants us all to truly participate in his compassion.

In multiplying the loaves and the fish, Pope Francis says, Jesus does perform a miracle—a miracle of love and compassion in response to great human need (Jesus can't just send all these tired people home without a meal). It's not a magic trick. In fact, he empowers his disciples to make it happen. In this way, Jesus is telling us that we all have a part to play in God's plan, and that it's up to us to get to work to make sure everyone is fed, everyone is noticed, and everyone is cared for. When we trust in God's trust in us, great things can happen.

PONDER

Do I have faith in God's trust in me?

PRAY

God of mystery and wonder, help me remember that you have made me to bring your light to others. Give me the tools to do so with joy!

9 | AUTHENTIC RECONCILIATION

*The Eucharist we celebrate transforms us
little by little into the body of Christ and spiritual
food for our brothers and sisters.*

It is impossible, says Pope Francis, to be a Christian
and to remain aloof from the needs of our brothers
and sisters everywhere. When we take the gift of the
Eucharist seriously, we are put into ever deeper rela-
tionship with others. When we are nourished at the
table of the Lord, we are filled with the Lord's power
and grace to share that goodness everywhere. Each
believer, Pope Francis says, becomes a servant of mercy, because Jesus wants to reach everyone. Through
our life in Jesus, we spread God's unconditional love.

PONDER

What does it mean to me to be part of the body of
Christ?

PRAY

God of mystery and wonder, open my heart to
receive your grace that I might share it gladly and
boldly with everyone!

10 | THIS IS THE PATH

*When Jesus saw the crowds, his compassion for
them led him to multiply the loaves for them;
he does the same for us with the Eucharist.*

Continuing his reflections on the story of the loaves
and the fish, Pope Francis reminds us that this miracle happens every time we come to Mass. We are
the crowds on the hillside looking for nourishment
after our tiring and often frustrating days. We are
the crowds hungry for a word of grace, a chance to
gather new strength in hopes of being better disciples in the week ahead. And sometimes we are
clueless and just hoping to hear and receive something that will help us make sense of our lives. Jesus
listens and responds to us; he heals and feeds us. The
miracle continues.

PONDER

What do I hope to receive from Mass?

PRAY

God of mystery and wonder, let me hear you,
let me see you, and help me witness to your love.

11 | YOU ARE SUFFICIENT

Solidarity must be our key word.
Though the world thinks badly of it, this ability
to make our humble capacities available to God is
what will make our lives fruitful.

It's easy to feel inadequate in our ordinary daily tasks—how much more so, then, at the thought of *living* the Eucharist in all that we do! Pope Francis tells us that the disciples felt the same way, but they were able both to get the crowd to sit down and also to feed them from their meager store of five loaves and two fish. When we all work together, we become stronger and all our individual gifts become a powerful force for good. Jesus will give us what we need, just as he does every time he feeds us.

PONDER

When I feel inadequate, do I still believe that God loves me?

PRAY

God of mystery and wonder, help me remember that you are always with me.

12 | THE GIFT OF EUCHARIST

Jesus gives us himself in the Eucharist to nourish us. When we accept and believe this gift, it transforms our life into a gift to God and to all we meet.

Pope Francis speaks often about what Jesus does for us in the Eucharist. Each time we come to communion, our God is present to us, and the bread and wine we offer are transformed by the Holy Spirit into his Body and Blood, just as we too are transformed more fully into his body. The Eucharist nourishes us and strengthens us to do God's work in the world. His gift to us becomes our gift to God—this gift that we can never fully understand or repay, but which we can come to appreciate more and more and use to God's greater glory.

PONDER

How often do I think of what Christ does for us in the Eucharist?

PRAY

God of mystery and wonder, help me to be aware of the great gift you give us in the Eucharist.

13 | THE BREAD OF LIFE

*When we permit ourselves to be nourished
by the Bread of Life, we are in tune
with the heart of Christ.*

It's comforting to think that we, with centuries of theological reflection and spiritual guidance to draw on, are probably still as much in the dark about the mystery of the Eucharist as were those who first heard Jesus identify himself as the Bread of Life. Pope Francis, in his customary simple language, makes clear what we *do* know: when we receive the Bread of Life at communion, we take on Jesus' divine life, his thoughts and actions, his behaviors and choices. This is a challenging undertaking, but Jesus tells us we are up to the task. All we need to do is believe.

PONDER
Am I ready to do what Jesus asks of me?

PRAY
God of mystery and wonder, my thanksgiving is equaled by my trepidation. Help me!

14 | ACTING IN JESUS' NAME

Receiving the Bread of Life means that we become persons of peace, forgiveness, and reconciliation.

Jesus does not give us the gift of himself so that we can hoard it for ourselves, Pope Francis says. Instead, it is meant to transform us into people who are filled with God's love and who act out of mercy and compassion, not out of a quest for power or domination. And we don't do this alone; we are meant to journey with others—to raise our voices and hearts with theirs—in solidarity and community. Peace, forgiveness, and reconciliation are often not popular words in today's world, because they might imply weakness. But, says Pope Francis, these are the words that give us our strength, because they were the principles that Jesus lived by. We can ask for no better model.

PONDER
How might I work for reconciliation in my life?

PRAY
God of mystery and wonder, fill me with your Spirit, so that I may do your work with joy!

15 | MADE PRESENT, HERE AND NOW

The Eucharist is not a private prayer or a beautiful spiritual experience. It is a gesture that makes present Jesus' death and resurrection.

Pope Francis reminds us that, when we come to Mass, we are not just remembering what Jesus did at the Last Supper. Rather, we are also taking part in his death and resurrection and following his call to take up his life in all that we do. It is his true Body and Blood that we consume—his everlasting gift of himself. It is not given to us as merely something to adore. Eucharist calls us to *action*, to do whatever we can to make Jesus' message heard by all those who need his blessing and grace.

PONDER

Do I know someone who needs to hear God's message? Am I strong enough to share it?

PRAY

God of mystery and wonder, give me courage and strength to follow your call wherever it leads me!

16 | ULTIMATE THANKSGIVING

Eucharist is the supreme thanksgiving to the Father, who so loved us that he gave us his Son out of love.

Eucharist means "thanksgiving," and, like so much else in the church, that definition has many levels. Pope Francis here is concentrating on Jesus' gift of himself to us, first proclaimed at the Last Supper, when he told his friends that the bread and wine they were consuming were his Body and Blood. There was no greater way to show his solidarity with us all—or to show us the kind of commitment we are asked to make as his disciples. We are praising God and giving thanks every time we receive our Lord—and every time the Eucharist leads us to give of ourselves, out of love, in our daily lives.

PONDER

How might I be more like Jesus?

PRAY

God of mystery and wonder, help me to understand and to emulate your endless love and compassion.

17 | ALL BECOMES ONE

*Word and bread in the Mass become one when
all Jesus' words and signs were condensed into
the gesture of breaking the bread and offering the
chalice, in anticipation of the sacrifice of the cross.*

Pope Francis brings together the two parts of our
liturgy when he speaks of the moment when Jesus,
the Word of God, asked his disciples to take and
eat, take and drink. In that one action, says Pope
Francis, Word and food came together, to become—
and to offer us—everything Jesus is and has done.
We repeat this action in each Mass, and we are asked
to live it outside the church doors, nourishing one
another with the words and signs and food of hope.

PONDER
Do the words I hear and pray at Mass make a
difference in my life?

PRAY
God of mystery and wonder, may my words be
yours whenever I speak!

18 | ALL MY BROTHERS AND SISTERS

At Mass we find ourselves with all sorts of men and women: young and old, poor and well-off, locals and strangers. Are these people my brothers and sisters?

Pope Francis asks us to consider our actions at Mass carefully. It is so important to him that we realize that at Mass we—all together—are being transformed into the *one* body of Christ, and that we are being called to give of ourselves as Jesus gave himself. Take a look around the next time you're at Mass—who's there you've never seen before? Who's there every week? Where do people sit? Do people make room for others? Do you? When this call to unity and service seems overwhelming, remember that God doesn't call the qualified. God qualifies the called.

PONDER

How welcoming am I to newcomers and strangers?

PRAY

God of mystery and wonder, help me to see your face reflected in everyone around me.

19 | A TRULY FRUITFUL LIFE

Do we let ourselves be transformed by Christ in the Eucharist? Do we let the Lord who gives himself to us guide us to going out ever more to give, to share, to love him and others?

Pope Francis believes in the power of Eucharist to transform us into people of mercy and love. We are asked to let Jesus work within us to change us, to open our hearts so that we may find no one a stranger, no one unworthy, no one irredeemable. We are asked to take the love we have been given and share it with all. When we do this, Pope Francis says, we join Jesus in being Eucharistic food for others. Accepting the Eucharistic meal that we share as the transformative gift it is—this is the key to a truly fruitful life.

PONDER
What one thing will I do today to share God's love?

PRAY
God of mystery and wonder, give me the strength and courage to be changed!

20 | PEOPLE OF EUCHARIST

*The Christian is a person who remembers
and celebrates the covenant.*

A Christian, a follower of Christ, is someone who "remembers," Pope Francis says. This means not just that we recall the stories and tenets of our faith, but that we apply them—by recognizing, accepting, and celebrating the gift of God's life in us and in all our brothers and sisters. A Christian is someone who is in constant contact with God, seeking to do God's will, remembering always God's covenant with us and our responsibilities because of that covenant. But God knows we are fallible, so he generously gives us the gift of the Eucharist to remind us always of the depth of his love in the Person of his Son. That's something to celebrate!

PONDER

Do I take time to remember God during the day?

PRAY

God of mystery and wonder, help me to see each action of the day as a way to bring you glory!

21 | A WILL TO SHARE

*Anyone who goes to the Eucharist without
having compassion for the needy and without
sharing is not modeling the actions of Jesus.*

The Eucharistic sacrifice, Pope Francis reminds
us, is nothing less than Jesus offering his life out of
love for us. By receiving this gift, we are called to
understand and embrace our own obligation to care
for the poor, the needy, the homeless, the rejected,
the sick, and anyone who is looked down upon by
society. What Jesus has done for us is what we must
do for others—love them, accept them, help them,
accompany them on their journey in life, and act out
of sacrificial love on their behalf. If we don't grasp
this, we are not following Jesus' path.

PONDER
What does receiving communion mean to me?

PRAY
God of mystery and wonder, I can never pay
you back for your blessings, but help me to be a
blessing to others in your name.

22 | BECOMING SPIRITUAL FOOD

Living communion with Christ is anything but being passive and detached from daily life; instead, we grow closer to everyone around us.

Understanding the Eucharistic sacrifice and our role in it goes beyond just thinking about what Jesus did, Pope Francis says. As we grow into "communion" with Jesus and with others, we ourselves become spiritual food for the world. If we take this call seriously, every encounter with Jesus in the Eucharist opens us up ever more to being of service to others. Jesus wants to be everywhere—and he *can* be, through us, his disciples. He uses us, as he used the loaves and fish, to feed the multitudes who surround us every day. We are called to be part of the miracle.

PONDER

Am I ready to accept my call to be of service?

PRAY

God of mystery and wonder, help me to grasp both the enormity and the simplicity of your call, and help me to do it well!

23 | RECOGNIZING JESUS' WOUNDS

The wounds of Jesus need to be heard!

Pope Francis suggests another image to bring this point home: "On the altar we adore the Flesh of Jesus; in the people we find the wounds of Jesus." We are all his wounds, especially the poor and needy. All these wounds cry out for justice and mercy, and we who receive Jesus' Body and Blood in the Eucharist are asked to be part of the healing. The Christian is one who learns to recognize the wounds of Jesus. Just as Jesus is hidden in the form of bread and wine, so is he hidden—yet present—in us and in all of our brothers and sisters everywhere, no matter how wounded we might be. Our communion with Jesus asks us to stand in solidarity with all.

PONDER
When was the last time I sought the face of Christ?

PRAY
God of mystery and wonder, open my eyes to recognize you in every moment!

24 | FOLLOWING JESUS

*In the mystery of the Eucharist, Jesus reminds us
every time that our life is not our own,
but rather a gift to him and to others.*

It is not too much, says Pope Francis, to speak of
our participation in the Eucharist as a personal and
intimate encounter with the Lord. Jesus' example
of unconditional love reminds us that the gift of our
own life was given to be used—and used well. We
are not to treat it like a possession, but to share it,
to give it back to God by giving it for others. This
kind of sacrifice asks us to say yes before asking why,
to agree to journey with another without asking the
destination, and to offer whatever we can that will
help. Through our human interactions, we are doing
divine work.

PONDER

Who needs my help today, and how do I start?

PRAY

God of mystery and wonder, remind me always of
the sacred trust you have in me.

25 | BECOMING RICHES

The Eucharist helps us understand that this road of service and sharing leads us to become riches through the power of God.

The power of God, Pope Francis says, is the power of love, and this love empowers us to be Eucharist for others. The little we have, he reminds us, like the few loaves and fish, can feed a multitude. God is always with us in a solidarity that, Pope Francis says, never ceases to amaze us. Indeed, when we actually pause to consider God's closeness to us—through the sacrifice on the cross and in every encounter in the Eucharist—we begin to see that we need not fear to follow Jesus' way. God will be with us, perhaps most visibly in the face of the next person we help.

PONDER

Where will I find Jesus today?

PRAY

God of mystery and wonder, may I see you today everywhere and in everyone!

26 | FROM THE VERY START

May God keep his presence alive in the church and shape our community in charity and communion, according to his heart.

How do we develop this willingness to belong to Jesus, to accept our call to be Eucharist for others? Pope Francis says it begins with our First Communion. The preparation for that moment, he says, must be thorough and engaging, so that young children begin to grasp what a life-changing step this is. Pope Francis says this moment is "the first step of this intense belonging" to Christ. And, once made, of course, it needs to be reinforced by the adults in a child's life who themselves accept every week this call to holiness and service.

PONDER
What do I remember of my First Communion? How has it influenced all my communions since?

PRAY
God of mystery and wonder, let me praise you each time I receive you!

27 | FROM CRADLE TO TOMB

When we live in concrete communion with Jesus through the Eucharist, we have already begun our passing from death to life.

The three sacraments of initiation—baptism, confirmation, and Eucharist—all work together throughout our life. In each of them we join Christ in death so that we might rise to new life in him. We receive baptism and confirmation only once, but Eucharist we can receive again and again. That's a good thing, says Pope Francis, because, being human, we need reminders along the way that our life is to be lived for others—all the way up to that day when we awaken after death and fully discover what this communion has been about all along.

PONDER
How is my participation in the Eucharist preparing me for eternal life?

PRAY
God of mystery and wonder, lessen my fear of death by reminding me of your resurrection promise!

28 | THROUGHOUT ALL CREATION

The Eucharist joins heaven and earth;
it embraces and penetrates all creation.

When Jesus gives us the gift of himself in the Eucharist and we pass that gift along to others in our daily lives, then, says Pope Francis, the circle of heaven joined to earth is complete—and it widens our focus. We may start our actions on a local level (as close by as our family and the people in the pews around us), but our call extends to embrace the whole earth and all of our brothers and sisters in pain or need. "The Eucharist," Pope Francis said in his encyclical *Laudato Si'*, directs us "to be stewards of all creation."

PONDER

How might I do more to care for the earth and all of the people who call it home?

PRAY

God of mystery and wonder, help me to celebrate all of your creation!

29 | LIFE AS GIFT

*Jesus' presence in the Eucharist is a life given
and one in which we share. When we
take and eat that Bread, we commit
to transforming our own life into a gift.*

Jesus comes to us in the Eucharist, Pope Francis
says, in order that we may ourselves become a gift to
others, especially the poorest and neediest. The call
to go forth at the end of Mass is just that—a sum-
mons to take the gift we have received and share it.
When we leave the church building, nourished and
(it is hoped!) filled with new purpose, this is where
our thanksgiving, our Eucharist, takes wing. As Jesus
gave his life for us, so we are to do for others. It's
perfectly fine to start small—sometimes an unbid-
den kind word or a smile is the best beginning of all.

PONDER
What way today will I celebrate communion?

PRAY
God of mystery and wonder, fill me with purpose
and energy to reflect your face to all!

30 | ACCEPTING THE MISSION

*The encounter with Jesus in the Eucharist becomes
the font of hope for the world if we accept the mission
to transform the world by showing God's love to all.*

Pope Francis says that when we accept our encounter
with Jesus in the Eucharist as a two-way street, we
allow ourselves to be transformed into nothing less
than "the image of the one we encounter" by the
action of the Holy Spirit. So we need never fear—we
can be confident that what we do can transform the
world, one person, one life, at a time. As St. Teresa of
Ávila put it so well, Christ has no body but ours on
earth to do his work. Knowing that in the Eucharist
we will always be fed, let us take up our call with
hope and joy!

PONDER
May I always seek to feel God's presence with me!

PRAY
God of mystery and wonder, fill me with courage
and conviction so that I may share your goodness
and love!